D1300655

COOL CAREERS WITHOUT COLLEGE FOR
PEOPLE WHO LOVE TO WORK WITH CHILDREN

COOL CAREERS WITHOUT COLLEGE FOR
PEOPLE WHO LOVE TO WORK WITH CHILDREN

HARRIET WEBSTER

The Rosen Publishing Group, Inc.
New York

Published in 2004 by The Rosen Publishing Group, Inc.
29 East 21st Street, New York, NY 10010

Library of Congress Cataloging-in-Publication Data

Webster, Harriet.
Cool careers without college for people who love to work with children/ Harriet Webster.— 1st ed.
    p. cm. — (Cool careers without college)
Summary: Explores the job descriptions, education and training requirements, salary, and outlook predictions for twelve careers that focus on children and do not require a college education.
Includes bibliographical references and index.
ISBN 0-8239-3792-5 (library binding)
1. Vocational guidance—Juvenile literature. 2. Occupations—Juvenile literature. [1. Child care—Vocational guidance.
2. Vocational guidance.] I. Title. II. Series.
HF5381.2 .W43 2003
331.7'02—dc21

2002012104

Manufactured in the United States of America

CONTENTS

CHILD CARE WORKER

Do you enjoy playing with young children? Do you take satisfaction in helping them learn new skills and explore new interests? Are you patient and sympathetic? If you answered yes to these three questions, a career as a child care worker may be right for you.

Child care workers are employed in a variety of settings. Some care for children in the child's home. Others work at a day care center or in the home of another caregiver. About 40 percent of child care workers are self-employed, taking care of children in their own homes. But wherever the setting, there is no more important job than taking care of the needs of children while their parents are at work.

If you have earned extra money working as a baby-sitter, you have already experienced a job as a child care worker. Your primary responsibility is keeping the child or children in your care safe and happy. As a child care worker, you will spend long periods of time taking care of children's basic needs, which may include preparing and serving nutritious snacks and meals, helping them to dress, helping them to stay clean and healthy, and making sure they get enough rest.

Some child care workers specialize in infant care. They are familiar with a baby's needs and know how to comfort a baby who is distressed. They also have enormous patience and are relaxed under pressure, as when an infant refuses to nap or cries for long periods of time. They prepare bottles and change diapers. They know how to hold an infant properly, and they are knowledgeable about which position an infant should sleep in. Most of all, the best child care workers in infant care are those who truly enjoy tending to babies.

More than most other jobs, it is vital that child care workers enjoy children and take pleasure in caring for them.

Child care workers engage the children they care for in activities that are fun and educational.

Because of the long periods of time they spend with children, they have a significant effect on the children's development. A good child care worker recognizes that part of his or her job is to encourage children's intellectual, social, and emotional development. Instead of sitting children in front of a television set for extended periods, a good child care worker plays games with them, reads books to them, takes them out for walks, initiates arts and crafts projects, and helps them to master skills like zipping their jackets or catching a ball. Child care workers who care for more than one child also need to teach children how to get along with others, and they need to understand how to best settle conflicts between children as well.

A competent caregiver respects the value of play in children's lives. She or he knows that building with blocks and doing puzzles are ways to introduce a child to basic math concepts. Similarly, making up stories, playing dress up, or joining an elaborate tea party complete with stuffed animal guests are all ways to stimulate language growth.

Another important part of a child care worker's job is to communicate regularly and effectively with the child's parents. They need to hear about problems that arise while the child is in day care. They need to be kept informed about the child's accomplishments and fears, as well as any behavioral issues that may arise. If you work in a day care center, there will probably be a set of rules or a specific routine that describes how to keep up communication with parents. For example, the center may send a notebook home with the child each day in which the child care worker notes any particular problems or developments in the child's life, and the parents write back with their comments, concerns, or questions. At other centers, parents and caretakers sit down together perhaps once a month to discuss the child.

While the majority of child care workers take care of children who are five years old or under, many others are employed in before- or after-school programs. They take care of elementary-school-age kids between the time their parents leave for work and school starts, or between the time school dismisses and the parents return home from work. While some caregivers mix full-time care of preschoolers with the before- and after-school care of older children, others choose to work part-time and do only the before- and after-school care. Some of these part-timers become full-time caregivers during school vacation periods, offering working parents a safe, fun place where they can leave their children while they are at work.

Education and Training

Education and training requirements for child care workers are different from one state to another. Each state has its own licensing requirements. In general, most child care workers with high school diplomas can find positions. Corporate day care centers and government-funded programs often have more demanding requirements. They may require a child care worker to have an associate's, or two-year, degree in early childhood education.

Salary

While pay is generally low for child care workers, additional education often means higher wages. Although

some day care centers offer benefits such as health insurance, the majority of child care workers do not receive much in the way of benefits.

Outlook

Both part-time and full-time jobs are available, and there are many opportunities. The relatively low pay leads to a large amount of turnover. According to the 2000 census, 712,000 people held salaried or hourly wage jobs in child care in 2000 in the United States, while 487,000 others worked as self-employed child care workers. The number of child care worker jobs is expected to increase rapidly over the next decade, since the number of working women between the ages of sixteen and forty-four continues to increase.

The number of day care centers is expected to grow as more states begin to require mandatory preschool for four-year-olds and as more corporations become involved in operating day care centers to meet the needs of their employees. Overall, there are likely to be many openings in this field.

Two child care workers take their charges for a stroll in the park. This important activity introduces children to the world beyond their homes.

FOR MORE INFORMATION

ASSOCIATIONS

American Red Cross National Headquarters, Health and Safety
18th and F Streets NW
Washington, DC 20006
Web site: http://www.redcross.org
Look up the local chapter in your community telephone book. Offers courses in child care and first aid.

Center for the Child Care Workforce
733 15th Street NW
Washington, DC 20011
(202) 737-7700
Web site: http://www.ccw.org
This organization works to improve the quality of child care services by improving the pay, working conditions, benefits, and training opportunities for family child care providers. Its Web site includes a series of free downloadable publications.

National Association for the Education of Young Children (NAEYC)
1509 16th Street NW
Washington, DC 20036-1426
(800) 424-2460
Web site: http://www.naeyc.org
Dedicated to improving the lives of children from birth through third grade, NAEYC is the country's most influential organization of early childhood educators. Membership is open to all. Its Web site includes a catalog of early childhood resource materials, including books, brochures, and videos, some in Spanish.

National Child Care Association
1016 Rosser Street
Conyers, GA 30012
(800) 543-7161
Web site: http://www.nccanet.org
This membership organization provides networking and professional development opportunities for people involved in childhood care and education. Here you can learn about the Certified Childcare Professional (CCP) credential.

WEB SITES

Early Childhood CDA Help
http://www.earlychildhood.cdahelp.itgo.com
This site is staffed by early childhood educators who teach at accredited state colleges. Here you can learn about online classes that count toward your child development associate degree (which is similar to the CCP). There is a list of materials you can purchase to help guide you through the CDA process. For a moderate fee, you can even correspond with a CDA adviser online as you work toward your credential.

COURSES

CARE Courses
P.O. Box 10526
McLean, VA 22102-8526
(800) 685-7610
Web site: http://www.carecourses.com
An international correspondence school, this company offers in-service training for child care providers working toward their CDA or CCP credential. All courses rely on books and materials that are transmitted through the mail. Its Web site lists the courses and gives clear descriptions of the steps necessary to acquire the credential.

Langara College
100 West 49th Avenue
Vancouver, BC V5Y 2Z6
Canada
(604) 323-5511
Web site: http://www.langara.bc.ca/programs/early-child.html
The school offers a one-year, full-time day program leading to a diploma in early childhood education, good preparation for work in day care centers and family day care situations. The site has links to Canadian regulatory agencies involved in the licensing of early childhood educators.

Mercer County Community College
P.O. Box B
Trenton, NJ 08690
(609) 586-4800
Web site: http://www.mccc.edu/degrees/pos/childcar.htm
This site lists courses required for the child care career development certificate, which can be used toward either a CCP certificate or a CDA degree.

VIDEOS

The Business of Family Child Care
The Soho Center
HC6 Box 612
Madison, VA 22727
(540) 923-5012
Web site: http://www.child2000.org/Video.htm
Produced by the nonprofit Redleaf Press, this video is available for $20.00. Or, ask your public library to request it.

Career Encounters: Early Childhood Education
Indiana Association for the Education of Young Children
P.O. Box 88474
Indianapolis, IN 46208-0474

(800) 657-7577
Web site: http://www.iaeyc.org/resource.htm
This video shows child care workers on the job in a variety of settings.
They talk about their work and provide a glimpse of high-quality early
childhood care.

BROCHURES

Love & Learn
National Association for the Education of Young Children (NAEYC)
1509 16th Street NW
Washington, DC 20036-1426
Web site: http://ww.naeyc.org
Straightforward approach to discipline techniques that respect young
children's feelings. Order item #528 (fifty cents).

2

COACH AND UMPIRE

Have you enjoyed playing organized sports since you were in the first grade? Is being on an athletic team your favorite part of school? Are you an avid sports fan? Is your mind an encyclopedia of sports rules and regulations? Do you enjoy teaching younger kids how to hold a bat or kick a ball? Do you feel extremely skilled and competent in one particular sport? If you answered yes to several of these questions, you might want to consider a career in coaching youth sports.

Our society's emphasis on health and fitness has nurtured the rapid growth of organized youth sports. Parents want their children to grow up active, and they want them to be well supervised. Participation in organized soccer and baseball leagues begins as young as six years of age, and many kids try out for competitive teams by the time they are nine. Along with increased participation comes greater opportunity.

Teams for beginning athletes are often coached by parents who are recruited not because they know about the particular sport but because someone needs to take on the responsibility. Parent coaches often welcome assistance from a teenager who plays that sport, knows the rules inside out, and is familiar with practice activities that can help beginners master the skills of the game. Offering to help out is an excellent way to get a taste of what coaching is all about. It also provides you with practical experience you can list on your résumé when you apply for a job in youth sports.

While the job of coach typically revolves around managing a team and utilizing players in the most effective way with the goal of winning, coaching a group of children is more about being a good teacher and a positive role model than about striving for victory. Through sports, children acquire new skills. They develop their gross motor (large muscle) skills and they also learn new social skills through their interaction with other players. In addition, they often become more fit and develop confidence and a positive sense of themselves.

As a youth sports coach, you must demonstrate specific skills and you will need to direct and correct young players without resorting to criticism that will discourage them. Patience, a sense of humor, and a positive, upbeat attitude are key components to becoming an effective coach when it comes to working with children. You should be prepared to deal with situations in which a group of kids make fun of a less capable child. You will need to figure out how to manage practices and games so that weaker players have the opportunity to improve and gain experience along with stronger players. And you will need to learn how to cope with parents who criticize your coaching style and second-guess your decisions.

Working with older children, including teenagers, involves many of the same problems and requires many of the same qualities as working with younger children.

A soccer coach enjoys his player's display of a newly learned skill. Coaches take a lot of pride in the development of their players' abilities.

But it also involves setting limits and imposing consequences without regard for the contribution a youngster
may make to the team's success. Preteens and teens are
at an age when they often test rules by breaking them. A
youngster who is caught smoking, for example, should be
penalized consistently whether he or she is a star or
merely an average player.

If you enjoy applying rules evenly, learning the fine
points of regulations, and making quick decisions under
pressure, you may want to try umpiring. In addition to the
capacity to make fast, fair calls under stress, umpiring
requires the ability to remain calm and clearheaded in the
face of criticism and heckling, which can come from players,
coaches, and spectators—parents in particular. Like
coaches, people who umpire youth sports need to always
remember that their primary role is to make certain that the
players have a positive experience unmarred by the behavior of those adults who take competition more seriously than
the well-being of the players.

Education and Training

The type and amount of education and training required of
coaches and umpires varies with the specific sport and the
level of play. Elementary and secondary schools often try
to hire their own teachers to fill coaching slots before

A baseball coach pulls double duty as an umpire during a community-league game.

hiring outside candidates. One of the most common ways to secure an entry-level part-time position—such as an assistant coaching job—is to begin as a volunteer, working with the paid coach. You can also get valuable experience by volunteering to coach or officiate for intramural or community leagues.

Depending on the sport, there are many organizations that offer the certification that indicates you have achieved a particular level of expertise. Most certification programs require experience in a camp, clinic, or school setting.

Salary

Earnings vary tremendously depending on educational level and certification. Many of the coaches who work in community sports with young children are unpaid. Those who coach teens often work part-time and are paid on an hourly or per-event basis. Of those who hold salaried positions in elementary and high schools, annual earnings are approximately $27,970. Those who work in recreation organizations like the YMCA can expect to earn about $23,000.

Outlook

Seventy percent of the people who held coaching, umpiring, and related jobs in 2000 held salaried positions, and nearly half of those worked in school settings. Most of the remaining 30 percent worked in gymnasiums, health clubs, golf and tennis clubs, karate schools, swim clubs, riding stables, and at related recreational facilities.

Jobs in this area are expected to increase about as fast as the average rate for all occupations over the next decade. Opportunities for those who want to work with young people are most often available to people interested in part-time coaching and umpire jobs at the high school level.

FOR MORE INFORMATION

ASSOCIATIONS

Coaching Association of Canada

141 Laurier Avenue West, Suite 300
Ottawa, ON K1P 5J3
Canada
(613) 235-5000
Web site: http://www.coach.ca
The mission of this organization is "to enhance the experiences of all Canadian athletes through quality coaching," touching on all sports and all levels. Provides a good source of information on the 3M National Coaching Certification Program (see Courses on the following page).

North American Coaching Schools Accreditation Agency

199-2805 East Oakland Park Boulevard
Fort Lauderdale, FL 33306-1813
This agency evaluates coaching schools according to fourteen specific criteria. Correspondence by mail only.

Pisgah Youth Organization (PYO)

P.O. Box 8093
West Chester, OH 45069
(513) 755-6500
Web site: http://www.pyobaseball.org/umpires/html
Anyone who wishes to umpire for PYO baseball games is required to attend its Umpire Certification School. Children twelve and up are permitted to umpire with parental supervision. The organization's Web site includes an example of the PYO's umpire test.

WEB SITES

Peer Resources
http://www.peer.ca/coachingschools.html
Features the names of dozens of coaching schools throughout the world, complete with the names of past participants who are willing to be contacted by e-mail. There is also good information on questions to ask when choosing a coaching program.

COURSES

Jim Evans Academy of Professional Umpiring
12741 Research Boulevard, Suite 401
Austin, TX 78759
(512) 335-5411
Web site: http://www.umpireacademy.com
Open to those eighteen years of age and older, this academy offers clinics as well as a five-week-long professional course.

3M National Coaching Certification Program
The Sport Alliance of Ontario
1185 Eglinton Avenue East
York, ON M3C 3C6
Canada
(416) 426-7053
e-mail: cclapp@sao.on.ca
Web site: http://www.coach.ca
More than 750,000 coaches have received training from this program since 1974. The five-level program meets the needs of beginning as well as accomplished coaches and is available to high school students as well as adults. Information on the high school portion is also available.

USA Coaches Clinics, Inc.
8420 Delmar, Suite 200
St. Louis, MO 63124-2177
(800) COACH-13 (262-2413)

Web site: http://www.usacoaches.com
Use the online catalog (or request a hard-copy catalog) to learn about instructional clinics around the country in a variety of sports. The company also sells a wide variety of videos, books, and software packages related to coaching. Sign up for their online newsletter.

BOOKS

NASPE Staff. *National Standards for Athletic Coaches: Quality Coaches, Quality Sports*. Dubuque, IA: Kendall/Hunt Publishing Company, 1995.
This book is the product of a project conducted by the National Association for Sport and Physical Education (NASPE), a branch of the American Alliance for Health, Physical Education, Recreation & Dance (AAHPERD). It describes a five-level program and thirty-seven standards that provide a basis for evaluating and certifying coaches that can be used by any organization. Available through the AAHPERD online store at http://www.aahperd.org.

Thompson, Jim. *Positive Coaching: Building Character and Self-Esteem Through Sports*. Portola Valley, CA: Warde Publishing, 1995.
Offers a good discussion focusing on the difficulties involved in coaching children. Filled with hundreds of constructive techniques for responding to the situations that typically arise in youth sports. Includes a wealth of stories that coaches can use to motivate their players and to develop strong communication skills.

PERIODICALS

Canadian Journal for Women in Coaching
Web site: http://www.coach.ca/women/e/journal
This online publication covers key issues and challenges faced by women coaches.

VIDEOS

Coaching the Spirit of Sport: Building Self-Esteem
Coaching Association of Canada
141 Laurier Avenue West, Suite 300
Ottawa, ON K1P 5J3
Canada
(613) 235-5000
Web site: http://www.coach.ca
This half-hour-long instructional video focuses on the role coaches can play in developing self-esteem in young athletes.

What Is Coaching All About?
This hour-long video features an in-depth discussion with some of America's finest coaches. For more information, e-mail usacoaches@aol.com.

3

ENTERTAINER

A large group of children sits in rows on the floor, wiggling and giggling with anticipation as the house lights dim and the stage lights are brought up. Two figures appear on the small platform at the front of the room, one lumbering painstakingly along on all fours with an enormous shell on his back. From the other side, an actor dressed as a rabbit emerges hopping energetically. So begins a performance of the beloved fable about the tortoise and the hare. During the next half hour, the audience of first and second graders will learn, through children's theater, that sometimes those who move slowly and steadily reach their goals before those who rush forward but then get distracted from their mission.

If you have developed your talent as a singer, dancer, actor, or other type of entertainer and enjoy performing in front of children, you might want to turn your hobby into a career. As a children's entertainer, you will perform in schools, youth centers, hospitals, day care centers, and summer camps, as well as at festivals and birthday parties.

Many people who work in this field write their own material, such as original stories, songs, and routines, or perform adaptations of old favorites. The material frequently teaches or sends a message appropriate to the age of the audience. The most sought-after performers are those who are in tune with the needs and interests of their young audience members.

To succeed in this career, you need to understand and enjoy children. That means recognizing that young audiences can sit still only for short periods of time. That is why many accomplished performers include in their routines opportunities for children to become involved in the performance. For example, a folksinger might encourage children to sing along or to "act out" a song with body motions, while a musician performing African tribal music might urge audience members to stomp their feet or clap their hands to mark the rhythm in a particular number. A clown or magician might ask for volunteers.

Children's performers work either independently or as part of a troupe. Many do both. As an independent performer, you will need to be a businessperson as well as an artist. You will need to publicize your act to get jobs. You will need to prepare a contract for each job that states your fee; the date, time, and length of the performance; and any other important details. You will also need to prepare and transport the necessary costumes, makeup, and props or scenery.

Most children's performers take up this career because they have been happily involved in the arts for a long time, often dating back to when they were young children themselves. If you find yourself attracted to a career as a children's entertainer, it is a good idea to participate in as many kinds of arts-related experiences as you can. For example, dancers should explore theater, actors should dabble in music, and clowns should explore ways to make music. The reason for this is that the more versatile you are as a performer, the more likely you are to be able to create an act that works with a variety of young audiences. Similarly, relying on your major instrument but also working several other instruments into your act will provide the kind of variety that holds a child's attention. If you are a puppeteer, preparing a show appropriate for preschoolers and another production geared to six- to nine-year-olds will enhance your opportunity to find engagements.

Earning a living as a children's performer is not easy. Part-time schedules are common and you will probably need to work frequently on weekends and holidays. You can also expect periods of on-and-off employment. It is particularly difficult to get a regular schedule of gigs (appearances) when you are just starting out. For this reason, many performers supplement their earnings with part-time jobs that may be completely unrelated to their work in the performing arts.

Some aspiring performers audition for theme parks that use children's entertainers, such as the Disney or Six Flags parks, both of which hire teenagers with experience in the performing arts. You might find yourself parading through the park dressed up as a popular character or participating in a song-and-dance extravaganza. It is all good experience, giving you a feel for how young audiences react and helping you to figure out how to best use your talents and personality in your work as a performer.

Education and Training

Although no formal education is required to become a children's entertainer, the more you know about your craft the

A group of children watches attentively as a clown performs a comical juggling act.

Disney costume characters entertain children at Walt Disney World in Florida. Performers must be cheerful, patient, and silent, even when they are not having a great day.

more likely you will be to succeed in this extremely competitive field. Take classes and lessons to strengthen your skills and to learn new ones. Sign up for workshops taught by experienced performers. Participate in high school and community productions whenever possible, accepting technical assignments like helping with costumes or working the lights as well as onstage opportunities. The idea is to get as much practice as you can in front of a live audience and to begin to network with people in the field who may be able to help you to land jobs.

You can also get experience by volunteering to entertain at a young cousin's birthday party or at a day care center or hospital. Begin to experiment with writing your own songs or skits. Read tons of children's literature. And be sure to make a point of attending performances by a broad variety of children's entertainers so you can get a sense of what works and what doesn't.

Salary

Salaried positions are difficult to find in this field. Many performers are paid by the appearance, and earnings are relatively low in general because of the downtime between engagements.

Outlook

There is a steady demand in this field that is likely to continue through, at least, the next ten years. One reason is that parents are increasingly eager to expose their children to the arts. Expanding satellite and cable television opportunities may also increase the amount of work available for children's entertainers. Although the competition is fierce, there will always be opportunities for new people to enter the field since many performers tire of the irregular hours and modest wages and eventually move on to other careers.

Duncan Wells, Children's Entertainer

Duncan Wells, a versatile and successful children's entertainer, has worked for over twenty years as a self-employed artist. He lives on Cape Breton Island in Nova Scotia with his wife and two daughters. Here are a few of his accomplishments and activities as a musician, songwriter, playwright, and actor dedicated to creating original material for children:

- Founded Duncan and the Apple in a Tree Band in 1990, a four-piece musical group that continues to perform for children and their parents.
- Produced three full-length albums of original songs for children.
- Developed a three-part program that teaches kids personal safety skills that can help to keep them from being physically or sexually assaulted, which he presented at all the elementary schools on Cape Breton Island.
- Launched *The Love and Safety Club for Children*, a live production of original songs.

- Worked with fifth- and sixth-grade students to produce *Welcome to the Club*, an original musical.

- Performed twenty-four shows in sixteen days in a tour sponsored by the Royal Bank of Canada.

- Received the first ever East Coast Music Award in the category of Children's Artist of the Year from the East Coast Music Association in 1995.

FOR MORE INFORMATION

ASSOCIATIONS
Clowns Canada
50465 Talbot Line, R.R. #1
Aylmer, ON N5H 2R1
Canada
(877) 368-7970 (for membership information)
Web site: http://www.geocities.com/clowncanada
Members of this organization include clowns, jugglers, magicians, face-painters, balloon artists, and other entertainers, most of whom live in Canada. Members receive a subscription to *Clowns Canada News* and opportunities to attend clowning workshops and conventions.

International Brotherhood of Magicians—Magical Youth International
11155 South Towne Square, Suite C
St. Louis, MO 63123-7813
Web site: http://www.magicyouth.com
Founded in 1922, the IBM is the world's largest organization of amateur and professional magicians. Membership in Magical Youth International is open to those twelve to eighteen years of age who have been interested in magic for one year. Members receive a quarterly publication called *Top Hat*.

International Storytelling Center
116 West Main Street
Jonesborough, TN 37659
(800) 952-8392
Web site: http://www.storytellingfoundation.net
The mission of this membership organization is to use storytelling to promote positive change in the world. Good source for workshops and courses on storytelling and information on the annual National Storytelling Festival.

WEB SITES

The Big Apple Circus
http://www.bigapplecircus.org
A one-ring circus in the classical European tradition, the Big Apple Circus has brought audiences across the country high-quality family entertainment since 1977. The site introduces special programs like the company's Circus of the Senses for hearing-impaired and visually impaired children and Beyond the Ring, which brings company members into schools to teach traditional circus skills.

Disney Careers
(800) 275-7404
http://disney.go.com/disneycareers/index.html
Filled with information on job opportunities. The company employs thousands of performers at its theme parks and resorts, and this site

provides information on auditions. Applicants must be at least eighteen years of age.

National Storytelling Network (NSN)

http://www.storynet.org

Dedicated to improving the quality of storytelling, the NSN provides educational workshops and sponsors the annual National Storytelling Conference each year. Its site contains valuable links to storytelling associations and events across the country. It also contains excellent information on how to get started as a storyteller.

Six Flags

http://www.sixflags.com/jobs/index.html

This site lists job opportunities for actors, actresses, jugglers, stilt walkers, and stunt and character performers sixteen years of age or older at Six Flags theme parks throughout the country.

COURSES

Priscilla Mooseburger

Box 700
Maple Lake, MN 55358
(800) 973-6277
Web site: http://www.mooseburger.com

A highly experienced educator in the art of clowning, Tricia Bothun has taught and performed around the country for the past twenty years. She created the clown character Priscilla Mooseburger, who teaches classes in character development, comic movement, clown band, makeup, and costume and character analysis. She also runs Mooseburger Camp, a weeklong summer session held in Maple Lake, Minnesota.

BOOKS

Kelly, Emmett. *Clown: My Life in Tatters and Smiles*. Cutchogue, NY: Buccaneer Books, Inc, 1996.
The autobiography of one of America's most famous clowns.

PERIODICALS

The New Calliope
The Blufton News
103 N. Main Street
Blufton, OH 45817
(712) 239-4599
Web site: http://www.coai.org
Published by Clowns of America International and distributed to members six times a year, this magazine contains a wealth of articles covering all aspects of clowning. It also includes sources for products clowns need and information on clown-related activities all over the country and worldwide. The Web site includes a detailed history of clowning.

Storytelling Magazine
National Storytelling Network
101 Courthouse Square
Jonesborough, TN 37659
(800) 525-4514
Web site: http://www.storynet.org/Magazine/mag.htm
Published bimonthly by the National Storytelling Network (NSN), *Storytelling Magazine* is available at no charge to NSN members. Single copies are $6.50 ($4.95 per issue plus shipping) to U.S. addresses.

4

FAMILY DAY CARE PROVIDER

A career as a family day care provider offers an excellent way to combine an interest in working with children with the desire to run your own business. Not only will you be responsible for taking care of the children's physical needs, including changing diapers, feeding, hand washing, and making sure they get enough rest, you will also want to provide them with a stimulating environment where they can progress socially and intellectually. In addition, you will need to attend to all the chores involved in operating your own business.

To begin, you will need to meet local and state licensing requirements. You will also want to determine how much to charge. You will need to set up an accounting system to keep track of your income and expenses. There are many responsibilities that come with running your own business. They include maintaining and cleaning your space, purchasing supplies and equipment, filing the appropriate taxes, and keeping records for each child (health forms, permission slips, and so on). Be ready to advertise your business and interview with parents who are interested in your service. In addition, it is important that you communicate regularly with the parents of the children in your care.

The most important part of your job is to provide each child with a safe, stimulating, and happy experience. Parents are not paying you to sit their child down in front of a TV. Occupying children in a meaningful way day after day requires lots of advance planning.

Competent caregivers prepare a daily schedule of activities that includes both quiet and active times as well as

Day care providers must always keep in mind the needs, tastes, sensitivities, and allergies of each child.

opportunities for both individual and group activities. If you are caring for children of varied ages, you will need to organize different projects for each age group. The more you know about child development, the better you will be able to engage children in projects that are well suited to their abilities.

Children learn best through play. By making available dress-up clothes, puppets, dolls, blocks, pots and pans, and other materials that encourage them to use their imaginations, you give children the opportunity to grow and learn. Creative activities like dancing, singing, painting, and putting on plays help children develop their language skills as well as build self-esteem. Taking walks in the woods or visiting nearby playgrounds are other types of activities to build into your schedule.

Working as a family day care provider can be physically tiring. Caring for infants and toddlers involves standing, stooping, and lifting. Keeping up with active preschoolers and keeping them safe requires energy and watchfulness.

On the plus side, caring for children in your home eliminates the need to travel to work. Nevertheless, in exchange for being your own boss, you give up some of your privacy by inviting children (and their parents) into your home.

Some experts in child development recommend no more than three or four infants (one year and younger), no more than five or six toddlers (one- to two-year-olds), and no more than ten preschool children (two- to five-year-olds) to a single caretaker. However, many parents prefer much lower numbers. State and local laws often specify the ratio of caretakers to children.

Education and Training

Each state has its own regulations regarding the licensing of family day care providers, but all require providers to have at least a high school diploma. As an independent family day care provider, the more experience and training you have, the more in demand you will be, and the more you can charge for your services.

Courses in early childhood development, first aid, nutrition, and the arts are all valuable to you. Consider getting an associate's degree in early childhood education through your local community college or apply for the nationally recognized child development associate credential awarded by the Council for Professional Recognition (see For More Information for details).

Salary

The more education a home day care provider has, the higher the earnings. Self-employed family day care providers do not earn a salary. Earnings vary according to how many hours the provider works and the ages and number of children cared for. Providers usually charge a higher rate for infant care.

A caregiver reads to two of the children in her care. Caregivers should always be mindful of finding new ways to engage children, who are likely to differ in personality and temperament.

Outlook

About two out of five day care workers are self-employed family child care providers. Over the next decade, there will continue to be a steady demand for qualified, licensed home child care providers for preschool children. As working parents become increasingly concerned about the quality of life and safety of their school-age children before and after school hours, there will be an increase in the demand for after-school care.

What Will It Cost?

Setting up a family day care program in your home involves some up-front expenses. Some of the items you will have to pay for include:

- Licenses and permits
- Health insurance
- Liability insurance
- Taxes
- Accounting and legal fees
- Equipment
- Furnishings
- Toys
- Arts and crafts materials
- Books
- Food
- First-aid supplies
- Outdoor play equipment
- Cots or pads for naps
- Fire alarms and extinguishers
- Increased utility and telephone bills

FOR MORE INFORMATION

ASSOCIATIONS

National Association for the Education of Young Children (NAEYC)
1509 16th Street NW
Washington, DC 20036-1426
(800) 424-2460
Web site: http://www.naeyc.org
According to its Web site, the NAEYC is the nation's largest and most influential organization of early childhood educators, working to provide high-quality programs for children from birth through third grade. Membership is open to all. The Web site includes detailed guidelines for choosing a high-quality early childhood associate's degree program.

National Association for Family Child Care
5202 Pinemont Drive
Salt Lake City, UT 84123
(801) 269-9338
Web site: http://nafcc.org
Provides detailed information on every aspect of starting your own family child care business, from applying for a license to purchasing insurance, from setting up a bookkeeping system to childproofing your home, and planning a daily schedule.

Wisconsin Child Care Resource and Referral Network
6314 Odana Road
Madison, WI 53719
(608) 271-1230
Web site: http://www.wisconsinccrr.org
Runs informational sessions about starting a day care business and offers training opportunities for potential child care providers.

WEB SITES

Child Care Aware
http://www.childcareaware.org
A nonprofit organization committed to helping parents locate quality care for their children. Site includes lots of information on issues important to parents and to family child care providers.

The Childcare Center
http://www.thechildcarecenter.com
Directed toward parents seeking child care, this site contains a list of the pros and cons of family day care.

The Children's Foundation
http://www.childrensfoundation.net
Organizing the National Child Care Program, they offer regional conferences about child care and child development. Each fall they hold a Child Care Training Institute in Washington, D.C. Each year they train hundreds of parents, family child care providers, nannies, au pairs, and center-based personnel on critical issues concerning the well-being of young children.

Daycare/Preschool—about.com
http://daycare.about.com
This site contains information on many aspects of family day care, including understanding regulations and how to make sure your program meets legal requirements. Lots of useful links to related services.

The Pediatric Group.
http://www.pediatricgroup.com
Provides information on ways to keep children safe and healthy.

COURSES

The Council for Professional Recognition
2460 16th Street NW
Washington, DC 20009-3575
(800) 424-4310
Web site: http://www.cdacouncil.org

Offers a nationally recognized child development associate credential to individuals who provide family child care. For providers who need training or experience before qualifying for the credential, the council offers a one-year training program, the CDA Professional Preparation Program.

Professional Career Development Institute (PCDI)
430 Technology Parkway
Norcross, GA 30092-3406
(800) 223-4542
Web site: http://www.pcdi-homestudy.com
PCDI is a home-study career school that offers practical, professional-level courses covering nearly fifty careers, including the Professional Child Day Care Program. Curriculum teaches about educational games, child growth and development, nutrition, socialization, first aid, and more.

BOOKS

Beauchemin, Cyndi L. *The Daycare Provider's Workbook*. West Linn, OR: TCB Enterprises, 1999.
This workbook is available by calling (503) 655-0457 or by ordering online from http://www.daycarehotline.com/contact.htm.

Gellert, S., K. Hollestelle, and E. Kotlus. *Helping Children Love Themselves and Others: A Professional Handbook for Family Day Care*. Washington, DC: The Children's Foundation, 1990.
This book, which contains a multicultural curriculum including activities designed to combat bias, is available by calling (202) 347-3300.

Hammond, Shannon. *A Day in the Life: A Keepsake Journal for Children in Daycare*. Lorton, VA: Jade Publishing, 2001.
This spiral-bound journal has spaces to record meals, naps, activities, and achievements. A good way for parents and providers to send brief notes back and forth to each other. Helps parents feel connected to their child's life away from home.

VIDEOS

I Am Your Child

I Am Your Child Foundation

National Association for the Education of Young Children (NAEYC)
A box set of six videos, twenty to thirty minutes each. Titles include
The First Years Last Forever (hosted by Rob Reiner), *Quality Childcare:
Making the Right Choice for You and Your Child* (hosted by Maria
Schriver), *Discipline: Teaching Limits with Love* (hosted by T. Berry
Brazelton), *Ready to Learn* (hosted by Jamie Lee Curtis and LeVar
Burton), *Safe from the Start* (hosted by Gloria Estefan), and *Your
Healthy Baby* (hosted by Phylicia Rashad). Available from NAEYC by
calling (800) 424-2460.

5

HUMAN SERVICE ASSISTANT

Human service assistants who work with children and teenagers fill a wide variety of jobs. Some work with young people who are physically disabled, while others work with children who are experiencing emotional difficulties. Still others do preventative work, reaching out to the community to provide assistance to youths that can help them avoid developing problems later on. Despite the differences in the populations they serve, what human service assistants have in common is a strong interest in improving the lives of their clients by helping them to solve problems and introducing them to opportunities.

In the world of human services, the word "client" refers to the person who is receiving services. Human service assistants provide their clients with both indirect and direct services. Indirect services refer to those tasks that don't involve spending actual time with the client. Often these tasks revolve around paperwork, like figuring out whether a child is eligible to receive a particular benefit. For example, if you work in a public welfare agency, you might examine a parent's tax return and related information to determine if a child qualifies for publicly supported health benefits.

Direct services refer to those tasks that involve actual contact with the child. Imagine that you work for a community center. Presenting children with different options for how they spend their after-school time and helping them to decide which program they would like to join is an example of direct service.

As a human service assistant in a community center, an important part of your job might be to provide your clients with a safe, supportive environment where they can discuss their concerns and explore healthy social and recreational

activities. If you work in a shelter, you might care for children while their mothers participate in counseling or job-training opportunities. As an employee at a residential facility, you might teach mentally retarded or physically disabled children to master independent living skills, such as bathing and dressing themselves.

Human service assistants work with children in a variety of settings, including residential facilities such as group homes or shelters. They also work in clinics, community mental health centers, community centers, day treatment programs, and psychiatric hospitals. Most work a forty-hour week and many spend their time on the road, visiting clients and their families at home. About a quarter of human service assistants work for state and local governments, mostly at public welfare agencies or facilities for clients who are mentally disabled or physically challenged.

Human service assistants often work closely with professionals such as social workers, psychologists, and psychiatrists. They help their clients participate in treatment plans designed by the professional staff, providing emotional support and encouragement along with instruction in areas such as how to communicate more effectively or how to behave appropriately.

A human service assistant watches as a disabled athlete participates in the Special Olympics in Cambridge, Massachusetts.

As a human service assistant, you may serve as an important link between the child and his or her family, communicating the child's needs, progress, and problems, and gaining insight into the child's background and requirements. Many workers report that the job is satisfying and gives a feeling of having really made a difference in a child's life. At the same time, the work can be emotionally draining, leading to a high turnover rate. Workers who take advantage of in-service training and other educational opportunities are rewarded with increased responsibilities and better pay.

Education and Training

While some employers require only a high school diploma, most prefer applicants with some post–high school education, such as an associate's degree or a certificate in human services or a related field. Community colleges often offer these programs, where students learn skills such as how to record information and conduct client interviews. They also practice problem-solving techniques and become familiar with crisis intervention procedures. Employers also look positively on high school graduates with relevant experience, such as working or volunteering at a summer camp or recreational program for disabled children.

Most employers offer their human service assistants ongoing in-service training opportunities. Employees with no education beyond high school are also likely to receive extensive on-the-job training at the start of employment. Human service assistants who work in group homes may be required to submit to a criminal background investigation.

Salary

In 2000, the median annual salary for human service assistants was $22,330. Those employed by state governments earned the highest salaries while those working for residential care programs earned the least.

Outlook

Job opportunities for human service assistants are expected to be plentiful over the coming years. At least until 2010, the number of available positions is expected to grow at a much faster rate than the average for other occupations. In fact, human service assistants rank as one of the most rapidly growing occupations. Many of these positions will involve working with the growing number of elderly people in our population. There will also be increased opportunity for human service assistants who provide help to pregnant teenagers, foster children and homeless children, young people with substance abuse problems, and children who live with physical disabilities.

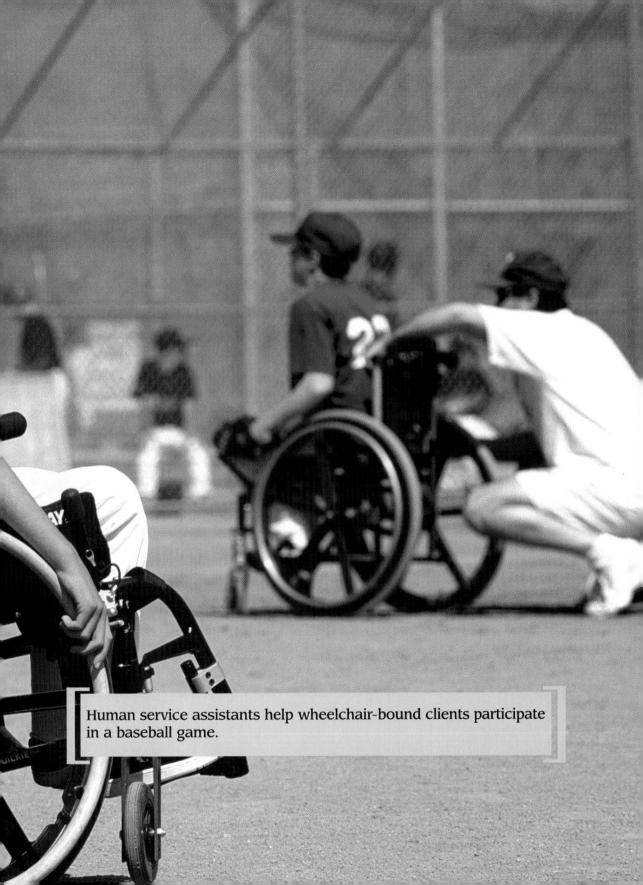

Human service assistants help wheelchair-bound clients participate in a baseball game.

Jobs for Human Service Assistants

Just as human service assistants have widely varied responsibilities depending on the setting in which they work and the characteristics of the population they serve, jobs for human service assistants have equally varied occupational titles. Here are some examples:

- Youth worker
- Residential counselor
- Drug abuse counselor
- Community outreach worker
- Special-needs care provider
- Community action worker
- Child advocate
- Child abuse worker
- Mental-health counselor

- Shelter worker
- Family support worker
- Behavioral management assistant
- Eligibility counselor
- Life-skills instructor
- Neighborhood worker
- Group activities aide
- Therapeutic assistant
- Group-home worker
- Intake interviewer
- Community organizer

FOR MORE INFORMATION

ASSOCIATIONS

The Child Welfare League of Canada (CWLC)
75 Albert Street, Suite 209
Ottawa, ON K1P 5E7
Canada
(613) 235-4412
Web site: http://www.cwlc.ca
The CWLC is a membership organization that promotes the well-being and protection of all children. The group's Web site offers solid information on programs and policies affecting Canada's most vulnerable young people.

The Council for Standards in Human Services Education
Northern Essex Community College
100 Elliot Way
Haverhill, MA 01830
This council is dedicated to improving the quality of human service training programs. It publishes a quarterly bulletin that describes current issues and trends in human service education.

National Center for Family Support at Human Services Research Institute
8100 SW Nyberg Road, Suite 205
Tualatin, OR 97062
(503) 885-1436
Web site: http://www.familysupport-hsri.org
This organization develops and distributes information about the best techniques available for providing support to families in need.

On its Web site, you can access policy briefs written in family friendly language that hone in on specific topics of interest to human service workers.

WEB SITES

Careprovider.org
http://www.careprovider.org
This site contains an employment search engine that allows users to explore job openings in the field of human services. Specify the city and state in which you would like to work, the ages of the clients you would like to work with, and the type of care you would like to provide. The program generates a list of job openings that satisfy your criteria.

The Child Welfare Training Resources Online Network
http://www.childwelfaretraining.org
This site contains sources of information on training opportunities for child welfare workers throughout the country. Select a state and find out what's available. In some cases, you can participate in a training session online.

National Organization for Human Service Education
http://www.nohse.com
This site offers information about the education and training of human service workers, and advocates for the development of creative approaches toward the teaching of skills required by those who work in the field.

Vinfen
http://www.vinfen.com
Vinfen is an easy-to-use site that presents an overview of the programs and job opportunities offered by a comprehensive private nonprofit human service organization in Massachusetts. Check out "Real Stories" to meet some human service assistants and hear about their experiences. Click "Vinfen Training Center" to learn about the in-service training opportunities offered to new employees.

BOOKS

Garner, Geraldine O. *Careers in Social and Rehabilitation Services*. New York: McGraw-Hill Professional, 2001.
Good information on careers working with juvenile public offenders and jobs that involve assisting young people struggling with physical, mental, or emotional disabilities.

Grobman, Linda, ed. *Days in the Lives of Social Workers: 50 Professionals Tell "Real-Life" Stories from Social Work Practice*. Harrisburg, PA: White Hat Communications, 1999.
This book allows readers to get an insider's look at the experiences of social workers in dozens of different settings. The chapter titled "Children, Youth, and Families" contains stories that will be of particular interest to anyone contemplating a career in human services with an emphasis on working with children and youth.

LIBRARY
ASSISTANT

It's 10 AM on a cold, gray Saturday morning. Orange, yellow, blue, and pink parkas are piled high on tables and chairs in the bright book-lined room. You sit on a thick rug surrounded by four- and five-year-olds. Some of them hold up picture books, anxious to convince you to read their choice. Others sit quietly waiting for the magic to begin. You urge them to quiet down. You ask them to close their eyes and to try to imagine the scene you are about to describe. Then you begin: "In an old house in Paris all covered with vines, lived twelve little girls in two straight lines."

By now your audience has quieted down. They have opened their eyes, too, eager to see the illustrations in the copy of *Madeline* you've chosen. One little boy asks where Paris is and you get up and fetch a globe. You show them where they live and you show them France. Then it's back to the story.

Welcome to the very best part of being a library assistant in the children's section. Working directly with children, you run a story hour, organize a holiday crafts session, or help kids learn to use computers to find the books they want to read. Other responsibilities might include setting up displays and bulletin boards or helping kids settle in at listening stations where they can hear music or a recorded story. You can help children with homework assignments requiring research. Library assistants who work in school libraries also help teachers locate the materials they need.

Being a library assistant may also involve a variety of clerical chores. Typical responsibilities include checking out books for young patrons, collecting overdue fines, processing new books before they are put on the shelves, reshelving returned books, and organizing magazines, pamphlets, and other materials. Library assistants also help to set up special events like puppet shows and programs presenting visiting authors and illustrators.

Library assistants who work in school libraries usually work a Monday-to-Friday schedule and have the same vacations as teachers. Those who work in public libraries work on a year-round schedule and often work some weekends and evenings.

Some library assistants serve as bookmobile drivers. They drive trucks or large vans stocked with books to patrons who may have difficulty getting to the library, including the elderly and people confined to hospitals. Bookmobiles often stop at schools (particularly those with no libraries of their own), day care centers, and other programs that cater to children, such as boys' and girls' clubs. Some bookmobiles even offer Internet access to users.

Education and Training

Training requirements for library assistants vary widely. Some employers require only a high school education, while others insist on an associate's degree. Good computer skills

A teenage volunteer library assistant reads to an elementary school student.

will also help you to land a job, as will experience working with children in summer camps or after-school programs.

If you are interested in this field, a good way to gain experience is to volunteer in your high school library or, better yet, explore volunteer opportunities at the children's department of your public library. Of course, volunteering to help out at your local public library on weekends while you are still in school is a great way to gain experience and develop library skills. It is also wise to familiarize yourself with popular children's books, both classics like *Madeline* and current favorites like the Harry Potter books.

Some community colleges and private two-year colleges offer an associate of arts degree in library technology. Library associations sometimes offer workshops and in-service classes focusing on new developments in library operations.

Salary

According to the 2000 census, the median annual salary for library assistants working in public school libraries was $21,120 in 2000. For those working in public libraries, the figure was $22,910.

Outlook

The number of library assistant jobs is expected to grow at about the average rate for all other types of jobs through

2010. While efforts to operate within tight budgets may mean that schools reduce the number of library assistants they can afford to hire, in some situations it may turn out that schools elect to replace librarians with library assistants to reduce costs.

The Newbery Medal, the Highest Honor in Children's Literature and Illustration

The Newbery Medal is the most important award given in children's literature. Named after an eighteenth-century bookseller named John Newbery, the Newbery Medal was the first children's book award in the world. Since 1922, it has been awarded to the author of the most creative and distinguished children's book of the year. How many of these medal winners have you read?

A Single Shard by Linda Sue (2002)

Holes by Louis Sachar (1999)

Number the Stars by Lois Lowry (1990)

Dear Mr. Henshaw by Beverly Cleary (1984)

Mrs. Frisby and the Rats of NIMH by Robert C. O'Brien (1972)

A Wrinkle in Time by Madeleine L'Engle (1963)

FOR MORE INFORMATION

ASSOCIATIONS

American Library Association—Association for Library Service to Children (ALSC)
50 East Huron Street
Chicago, IL 60611
(800) 545-2433
Web site: http://www.ala.org/alsc
The oldest and largest library association in the world, the ALA is committed to the development and improvement of all aspects of library services. Membership is open to anyone who works in or supports libraries. Members of ALSC, which is a division of the American Library Association, include library assistants who work with children and children's librarians.

Manitoba Library Association
606-100 Arthur Street
Winnipeg, MB R3B 1H3
Canada
(204) 943-4567
e-mail: info@mla.mb.ca
Web site: http://www.mla.mb.ca
Contains information on library careers in Manitoba.

New York State Library Assistants' Association (NYSLAA)
SUNY Geneseo
Milne Library
1 College Circle
Geneseo, NY 14454-1498
(716) 245-5594, ext. 2

Web site: http://nyslaa.org
The NYSLAA is an organization for library assistants run by library assistants. It offers a certificate of achievement program that recognizes the contributions of career-oriented library assistants. Certificates are awarded on four different levels, each one indicating an increasingly demanding level of achievement. Points toward certification are awarded for experience, formal education, and participation in workshops, conferences, and other professional development activities.

WEB SITES

The Children's Literature Web Guide
http://www.ucalgary.ca~dkbrown
Chock-full of information about children's literature, including many links to resources for storytellers, parents, teachers, and writers. Also covers books for young adults.

The Librarian's Guide to Cyberspace
Web site: http://www.ala.org/parentspage/greatsites/guide.html
Created by librarians, this site selects, organizes, and categorizes Internet information to help children make their online time useful and safe.

COURSES

ALA Is Continuing Education
Web site: http://www.ala.org/hrdr/alaisc.html
This brochure describes dozens of workshops and conferences that provide continuing education for people who work in libraries. Events are held throughout the year in many different parts of the country.

Council on Library/Media Technicians (COLT)
PMB 168
28262 Chardon Road
Willoughby Hills, OH 44092
Web site: http://colt.ucr.edu
COLT's Web site contains an excellent listing of U.S. library technicians programs in the United States and Canada. Includes certificate programs as well as associate's and bachelor's degree programs.

BOOKS

Mathews,Virginia M., and Susan Roman. *A Library Head Start to Literacy: The Resource Notebook for the Library–Museum–Head Start Partnership.* Washington, DC: Library of Congress, Center for the Book, 1999.
At nearly 300 pages, this invaluable volume stresses family literacy through collaborations with librarians and museum specialists who serve children.

VIDEOS

ALA Library Video Network
320 York Road
Towson, MD 21204-5179
(800) 441-8273 (ask for catalog)
Offers over eighty-five video titles designed to be used for professional development, including several that focus on children's library services and children's videos.

MUSIC, DANCE, OR ART TEACHER

Parents want the best for their children. One of the ways they try to help their kids flourish is to provide them with plenty of enrichment activities. These activities revolve around opportunities to learn new skills and explore their creativity. If you have become competent in one of the arts, you may want to pass your knowledge on to young students by working as a music, dance, or art teacher. While people who teach these skills in a school setting must have a college education and teaching credentials, those who teach in studios, music stores, community centers, private homes, and after-school programs do not have to meet these requirements.

In order to do well in this field, you must be accomplished in the area you plan to teach. Whether you want to offer lessons in piano, violin, ballet, tap dancing, painting, or ceramics, you need to feel absolutely confident in your ability. You must also be a competent teacher, with a whole different set of skills from those involved in being an artist. No matter how gracefully you dance, you will not succeed as a dance teacher unless you can excite your young students about the subject they are there to learn.

Good teachers present lessons in a variety of forms both to keep their pupils interested and because different children learn in different ways. The ability to explain an idea or procedure, to demonstrate a skill, and to break a challenge down into small manageable steps are all parts of being a good instructor. So, too, is the ability to make the lesson fun.

It is also important to recognize that your young students may have a whole range of attitudes toward taking lessons.

An art teacher watches as her student paints. Art teachers should not only be competent artists, they should also be skilled in explaining techniques and concepts in ways that children understand.

Let's say that you are a piano teacher starting out with three seven-year-old students. One child may be tremendously eager to take lessons. Another might have signed up only because his parents think the experience will be good for him. A third child might have enrolled because her best friend is taking lessons and she doesn't want to be left behind. As a teacher, you need to accept each child's agenda and recognize that many children sample a variety of enrichment activities before finding one that they really enjoy.

Enrichment teachers usually see each child once a week. Music teachers most often give private lessons, while dance and art teachers customarily give group lessons. Each session must be carefully planned with clear objectives and a variety of activities.

It is also important to listen attentively to your students. The pleasure a child gets out of an enrichment activity is often directly related to the quality of the relationship the child has with the teacher. The more you encourage and support your students, the harder they will work to master the skills you are teaching and the more they will enjoy learning from you. At the same time, a good teacher does not focus on mistakes but instead pushes young students to experiment and explore as they discover their own creativity.

Most parents are realistic enough to realize that their child is not likely to turn out to be a Mozart, a Martha Graham, or a Picasso. They recognize that enrichment lessons have lots of advantages whether or not their child becomes proficient. Through their participation, children develop coordination, physical strength, the ability to concentrate, a sense of discipline, and a sense of themselves. They may also develop an appreciation of the arts and a lifelong hobby that gives them pleasure. Or, they may grow up to be professionals.

Enrichment teachers who concentrate on preschoolers frequently offer morning classes. Those who focus on older children usually work around school hours, scheduling lessons in the late afternoon, on weekends, and sometimes in the evening.

Education and Training

The most important credential enrichment teachers need is a thorough grounding in the subject they want to teach. Many teachers are students themselves. That is, they continue to take lessons to improve their own skills. Your teacher can also offer you valuable advice as you begin to deal with your own pupils.

In addition to your specialty, you should have a working knowledge of your field. If you specialize in piano, for example, you should also become competent at playing several other instruments. Similarly, a ballet instructor should be familiar with styles of dance like jazz, tap, ballroom, and hip-hop. A painter who teaches children's art classes should know how to work in clay and collage.

A ballet instructor leads her students through a series of important exercises.

Salary

While some enrichment teachers are employed by community organizations and after-school programs, most are self-employed. Most charge an hourly rate, which increases as they develop experience, a reputation, and a clientele. That rate typically ranges from $20 to $60 an hour for private instruction. Instructors who teach classes usually charge one-third to one-half as much per pupil.

Outlook

Several trends combine to create a positive outlook for enrichment teachers. First, as the level of education rises in this country, parents are increasingly looking for ways to give their children more opportunities to develop their talents. Second, as public schools experience budget cutbacks that often translate into fewer arts programs, parents try to replace lost opportunities by providing their children with enrichment experiences outside of school.

Five Ways to Get Experience as an Enrichment Teacher

- Ask a parent in your neighborhood if you can give their child lessons free of charge for six weeks. You will gain experience and possibly a good reference when you try to recruit paying students.
- Ask an established art or dance teacher if you can assist with group lessons.
- Offer to give group lessons to a Girl Scout troop that wants to earn a badge in your area of expertise.
- Volunteer to teach at an after-school program.
- Get a summer job as a camp counselor where you can offer instruction in your specialty as one of the camp's activities.

FOR MORE INFORMATION

ASSOCIATIONS

American Dance Guild (ADG)
P.O. Box 2006
Lenox Hill Station
New York, NY 10021
(212) 932-2789
Web site: http://www.americandanceguild.org
The ADG serves the needs of performers, choreographers, teachers, and students through all stages of their careers.

National Art Education Association
1916 Association Drive
Reston, VA 20191-1590
(703) 860-8000
Web site: http://www.naea-reston.org
A membership organization of over 17,000 art educators, parents, and students. Publishes a newsletter focusing on research and issues affecting art education.

The National Association for Music Education
1806 Robert Fulton Drive
Reston, VA 20191
(800) 336-3768
Web site: http://www.menc.org
The mission of this organization is to encourage everyone—young and old—to study and play music. The site includes information on music from different parts of the world along with teaching materials, contests, and musical games.

WEB SITES

The Drama in Education Site
http://www.stemnet.nf.ca/~mcoady
Produced in Canada, this site is for people who teach drama. It has good resources for those who live in Newfoundland and Labrador.

National Dance Education Organization
http://www.ndeo.net
This organization works to promote excellence in dance education both in schools and in private studios.

COURSES

Canadian Children's Dance Theatre
509 Parliament Street
Toronto, ON M4X 1P3
Canada
(416) 924-4141
Web site: http://www.ccdt.org
This modern dance repertory company is made up of gifted dancers, twelve to eighteen years old, who perform all over the world. The School of the Canadian Children's Dance Theatre & Youngstudios offers young people classes in creative dance, ballet, modern, jazz, tap, and hip-hop. Student teacher internships are available.

Luna Kids Dance
P.O. Box 8058
Berkeley, CA 94707
(510) 644-3629
Web site: http://www.lunakidsdance.com
This group strives to empower children and to spark their creativity through dance. Dance is viewed as a tool that can help children to develop self-esteem, tolerance, and understanding. Luna Kids Dance offers workshops and courses for teachers who want to inspire children.

MusicStaff
Web site: http://www.musicstaff.com
This site contains a section of online lessons where music students can access tips and advice from some of the world's best music teachers along with interactive lessons. There is also an active discussion board where music teachers share opinions and ideas.

BOOKS

Purcell Cone, Theresa. *Teaching Children Dance: Becoming a Master Teacher*. Champaign, IL: Human Kinetics, 1994.
Contains seventeen dance activities (called "learning experiences") that teachers can use with children as young as four years old. A companion video, also available, shows real-world examples of teachers effectively presenting the lessons to children.

PERIODICALS

DanceTeacher
Lifestyle Ventures
250 W. 57th Street, Suite 420
New York, NY 10107
(212) 265-8890
Web site: http://www.dance-teacher.com
Written for professional dance instructors, this magazine includes articles on all aspects of dance education, including teaching techniques, costumes, and training programs.

Plays: The Drama Magazine for Young People
Kalmbach Publishing Company
21027 Crossroads Circle
P.O. Box 1612
Waukesha, WI 53187-1612
Web site: http://www.playsmag.com
Produced monthly from October through May each year, this magazine publishes over sixty original plays for children.

VIDEOS

Centralhome Active Videos
10 First Avenue E
Mobridge, SD 57601
(800) 342-4320
Web site: http://www.centralhome.com
Its Web site lists videos that demonstrate dance instruction techniques for styles that include hip-hop, hula, swing, tap, ballet, and ballroom. Sample titles include *Baby Ballet*, *Bob Rizzo's Ballet Class for Kids*, *Ballet for Boys*, and *Junior Jazz*.

NANNY

Did you ever read *Mary Poppins*, P. J. Travers's famous novel about a British nanny with magical powers who flew in on the wind to take care of the Banks children? Of course, being a nanny is a serious and responsible job, but there's a lesson to be learned from Mary Poppins: A good nanny knows that encouraging children to explore their creativity is an important ingredient of success.

Unlike child care workers, nannies care for children in the children's homes. Unlike baby-sitters, nannies spend prolonged periods of time with the same family. Some nannies "live in," meaning that they have a room and a bathroom (sometimes shared with the children) in their employer's home. Others "live out" and come to work each day for a set period of time.

If you enjoy working with children, are patient, have a sense of humor, and use common sense, you already have some of the chief qualifications required to be a nanny. A nanny also needs to be able to communicate clearly with both children and parents. It is critical to understand that children have different needs at different ages. If you have all these attributes and are also organized and respond well in an emergency, this might be a good career choice for you.

Working as a nanny is demanding. You may be on duty up to sixty hours a week. You will have to adjust to living in someone else's home and you may give up some of your privacy. You will be completely responsible for your employer's children, caring for them when they are sick, getting them to their play dates and activities, preparing their meals, doing their laundry, making certain they get their homework done, disciplining them when necessary, and offering comfort and companionship. You should not, however, be asked to do general housework; that's not your job.

Most families in search of a nanny are looking for a good match. They want to hire someone who is comfortable with children the ages of their kids (taking care of an infant is very different from taking care of a six-year-old). Employers want to find someone who fits in with their family because a nanny does in fact become a part of the family. They also want to find someone who will make a commitment to stay for a set period of time, usually a year.

As a potential nanny, you are looking for the right match, too. The key to finding a good situation is to ask lots of questions and to take the time to get to know both the parents and the children before making a commitment.

Once you have found a position, ongoing, clear communication is absolutely essential to avoid misunderstandings and the problems that can develop from them. Since the duties of a nanny vary greatly from one job to another, it is best to have a written agreement with your employer describing your responsibilities and privileges.

Many nannies perform most of the typical parenting functions. As a result, they often form powerful bonds with the children they raise and are often considered integral parts of the families they serve.

Education and Training

Child care workers can generally find employment with a high school diploma and little experience, but nannies are usually held to a higher standard. While most families prefer to hire nannies with some training and experience in caring for children, the reality is that—because of the heavy demand for nannies—many have no previous training or experience.

High school courses in child development are a good way to begin to prepare for a career as a nanny. Extensive baby-sitting experience is also a plus, as is any other work that involves children, such as employment as a camp counselor. Many families will also expect you to hold a driver's license and to have a good driving record.

Schools that train nannies offer courses in early childhood education, nutrition, and child care. Training programs in the United States offer basic six-week programs, one-year certification programs, and college programs offering an associate's or bachelor's degree.

Salary

Salaries for nannies vary widely, according to the part of the country where the nanny is employed and according to the qualifications and experience the individual nanny brings to the job. Starting salaries range from $250 to $400 per week,

A nanny helps a group of children complete jigsaw puzzles at the Norland Nanny School in Berkshire, England. Training programs include courses on child care, nutrition, and early childhood education.

while a trained nanny can make as much as $1,000 per week. In addition to salary, live-in nannies receive free room and board.

Outlook

Since the number of children under five years of age is expected to grow between 2000 and 2010, the demand for child care workers in general is likely to continue to increase. This trend, combined with high turnover, should create ample opportunities in the field. Nannies are usually employed by families that are financially comfortable. There appears to be a continuing need for competent nannies among affluent families, particularly single-parent families and those in which both parents work.

People Who Care for Children in the Children's Homes

Governess

A well-educated person with a solid child care background who provides academic instruction in the home (like Miss Anna in *The King and I*). A governess usually does not provide care for infants or do housework.

Nanny

A person who is employed by a family to take care of one or more children in their home. Responsibilities are limited to child care and household tasks that are directly related to the children, like preparing their snacks, doing their laundry, and helping them straighten their rooms. A nanny usually works without supervision.

Mother's Helper

A person who provides full-time child care and household help for families in which one parent is usually home. A mother's helper often cares for one child while the mother is involved with another child. He or she is sometimes left alone with the children for short periods of time.

Au Pair

Someone who lives with a family and helps out with child care and light housework, under the supervision of parents. Au pairs usually seek placement in a foreign country (an American teenager going to France or a French teen coming to the United States, for example). They receive a small stipend and the opportunity to experience life in a different culture.

Baby-Sitter

Baby-sitters care for children on an irregular basis.

FOR MORE INFORMATION

ASSOCIATIONS

International Nanny Association
900 Haddon Avenue, Suite 438
Collingswood, NJ 08108
(856) 858-2519
Web site: http://www.nanny.org
Membership in this nonprofit association is open to all those who educate, employ, or place professional home child care providers. The Web site includes an excellent online brochure, "So You Want to Be a Nanny," which answers the questions people most often ask about entering this field.

WEB SITES

4Nannies.com
http://www.4nannies.com
This placement agency's site contains an online job application. It also includes an excellent question-and-answer section with detailed answers. There is also a section on how to improve your chances of getting a job.

4Nannytraining.com
http://www.4nannyschool.com
This site includes a free interactive self-assessment test that can help you identify your strengths and weaknesses as a candidate for a job as a nanny. The multiple choice quiz takes about forty-five minutes to complete and covers subjects like safety and discipline, nutrition and meal planning, and early childhood development.

Nannies Plus
http://www.nanniesplus.com
This child care referral agency matches nannies with families looking for live-in child care providers all across the United States. Provides guidelines for evaluating nanny agencies found on the Internet.

The Nanny Authority
http://www.nannyauthority.com
This nanny agency's site includes specific information on every aspect of a nanny's job, from work schedule to responsibilities to salary and expenses.

NAN Web Page
http://www.nannyassociation.com
National Association of Nannies. This is an organization run by nannies who are dedicated to promoting high-quality caregivers in America.

NannyNetwork.com
http://www.nannynetwork.com
An excellent list of organizations in twenty-five states that provide social activities, professional development, and networking opportunities for nannies.

COURSES

The Nanny Training Institute
(800) 777-1720, ext. 114
The Nanny Training Institute gives eight-hour-long workshops at locations across the country. Practicing nannies who are new to the profession learn how to communicate effectively with employers and how to develop daily routines that are appropriate to the child. If you can't attend the course, you can order the Nanny Kit, which contains the workbook from the workshop, a book covering child

development from birth to age five, and a video focusing on the first years of life.

Northwest Nannies, Inc.
11830 SW Kerr Parkway, Suite 100
Lake Oswego, OR 97035
(503) 245-5288
Web site: http://www.nwnanny.com
Northwest Nannies Institute offers a thirty-week training program that combines classroom work with hands-on experience working with children and families.

BOOKS

Bassett, Monica M., RN. *The Professional Nanny*. Florence, KY: Delmar Publishers, 1998.
Describes the nanny as a child care professional responsible for the physical, social, and emotional well-being of children.

Waterman, Pamela. *The Absolute Best Play Days*. Naperville, IL: Sourcebooks, Inc., 1999.
Chock-full of activities for four- to nine-year-olds. Includes crafts, music, videos, and indoor and outdoor activities, all grouped according to themes.

ARTICLES

"How to Nanny Successfully with Difficult Children," by Dorothy Popovich. http://www.nannynetwork.com/NannyDifficultChildren.html
Reprinted from NaniNet, Inc, this is a detailed discussion covering the many causes of difficult behaviors and approaches to addressing them. Includes information on setting and enforcing rules and on discussing the problem behavior with the parents and the child.

"Other People's Kids...Words from the Nanny," by Charlotte Macchia.
http://www.thelaboroflove.com/forum/nanny
Experienced nanny Charlotte Macchia lives in Winnipeg, Manitoba,
and writes an online newsletter that contains friendly, personal articles
about the many sides of the nanny experience.

RETAILER

Imagine yourself helping a customer who is searching for just the right birthday present for a six-year-old who loves crafts. Picture yourself explaining the pros and cons of different kinds of in-line skates to a nine-year-old and his mom. Now think about what advice you would offer to a shopper trying to decide whether to purchase a

96

one-piece or two-piece snowsuit for her two-year-old grandchild.

If you think you would enjoy these types of situations, you might be suited to a job in retailing, specializing in the sale of products used by children. These positions are available in department stores as well as in toy stores, sporting goods stores, and stores that specialize in children's clothing.

The major job of a salesperson is to deliver customer service. This means interesting customers in age-appropriate products and answering their questions. That's why it's important to be knowledgeable about both the items you are selling and the person who will eventually use a particular product. For example, the more you know about child development, the more successful you will be in helping parents or grandparents choose the right toy.

People who enjoy kids make good salespeople in stores that sell products for youngsters because parents often take their children along when they shop. If you are patient and pleasant, customers will feel more comfortable and will be more likely to buy. Some toy stores have activity centers where kids can play while their parents shop. A sales associate with experience in child development may be assigned to supervise the center. Other stores encourage salespeople to demonstrate how different products work. In the end,

whether you are selling basketballs, board games, or boots, your ability to help the customer find the product most appropriate for his or her child is what will determine your success in this field.

In general, salespeople spend long hours on their feet and often do physical work such as lifting boxes, stocking shelves, and moving merchandise. The work setting is usually clean and well lit. Salespeople are expected to help keep merchandise organized and attractively displayed.

Another important aspect of the job is that salespeople are often responsible for handling large amounts of money. They ring up sales on a cash register or electronic terminal and handle returns and exchanges. They may also be responsible for making deposits and ensuring that at the end of the day the contents of the register match the quantity of sales made.

Many of the people who work in this industry hold part-time jobs. Since weekends are particularly busy shopping times, salespeople need to be willing to work on Saturdays or Sundays. Employers also often require evening hours and extra hours around holidays.

A sales associate demonstrates a train set to an interested three-year-old.

Education and Training

Most entry-level sales jobs do not require formal education, but many employers prefer to see a high school diploma. Proficiency in English is often required; some larger employers offer language training for applicants who need assistance. Applicants who have taken high school courses such as marketing, accounting, and business math are likely to be looked at favorably by potential employers.

If you would like to work in a sporting equipment store, your experience playing a variety of sports and your ability to talk intelligently about the equipment related to those sports is an important part of the "education" you bring to the job. Similarly, if you are seeking a job in a toy store, a résumé that lists courses in child development is likely to catch an employer's eye.

Salespeople almost always receive on-the-job training. In smaller stores, the manager or an experienced salesperson will provide instruction on how to process cash, checks, and charge sales, as well as how to use the cash register. You will also need to learn how to handle returns and special orders. In larger stores, new employees participate in more formal training programs that last several days. In addition to learning about customer service, store policies, and security procedures, participants may receive training related to the particular type of products they will be selling.

Although it is still possible for competent salespeople to be promoted into the managerial ranks without a college degree, an increasing number of retailers prefer to promote workers who have taken college courses in marketing, merchandising, or business. Computer skills are also highly valued. Taking courses in these areas at a community college while you are working in retail can improve your opportunities for advancement.

Salary

Retail workers in nonsupervisory positions earn less per hour than workers employed in private industry. Larger stores usually offer more comprehensive benefits than do smaller stores. Most employers allow workers to purchase merchandise at a discount.

Outlook

Opportunities in this field are available throughout the United States and Canada. While the number of sales jobs is expected to increase at a slower than average rate from 2000 to 2010, job openings are expected to be plentiful because of the large amount of turnover. Young workers seeking their first job are likely to find positions.

The Ideal Retail Job–Seeker Should Possess the Following Qualities:

- People skills: understanding of the customers' wants and needs; serving them well and enthusiastically; getting along with your fellow employees.

- Flexibility: able to adjust in an ever-changing global retail marketplace; interacting with many people on different levels; performing a wide variety of tasks during the workday; being resourceful.

- Decisiveness: self-motivated and self-starting; able to make quick, calculated decisions; follow through with responsibilities; accept responsibility for your results.

- Analytical skills: solving problems, analyzing data and predicting trends; establishing priorities; familiarity with technologically advanced tools for managing infrastructure.

- Stamina: perform well under pressure; maintain professional standards under varied work conditions.

(Source: National Retail Federation, http://www.nrf.com)

FOR MORE INFORMATION

ASSOCIATIONS

Distributive Education Clubs of America, Inc. (DECA)
1908 Association Drive
Reston, VA 20191
(703) 860-5000
Web site: http://www.deca.org
DECA is dedicated to improving student education and career opportunities in marketing, management, and entrepreneurship. With 180,000 student members and faculty advisers, this student organization is associated with over 5,000 marketing education programs at high schools and colleges across the United States and Canada.

National Retail Federation
325 7th Street NW, Suite 1100
Washington, DC 20004
(800) NRF-HOW2 (673-4692)
Web site: http://www.nrf.com
This membership organization offers information and events on all aspects of retailing. Its Web site includes excellent descriptions of the career paths in retailing open to those with at least a high school education, and the opportunities for advancement offered in each one.

WEB SITES

DECA Ontario
http://www.deca.on.ca/index.html
Through membership in DECA, 2,400 students from fifty-three Ontario high schools learn communication, human relations, and employability skills important in a retailing career.

KB Toys

http://www.kbtoys.com

A retailer specializing in mall-based stores. Its Web site offers detailed descriptions of assistant store manager and store manager positions, including job responsibilities and qualifications.

OshKosh B'Gosh

http://www.oshkoshbgosh.com

Headquartered in Oshkosh, Wisconsin, OshKosh B'Gosh is known worldwide for its high-quality products for children, from newborn to ten years of age. This site outlines career opportunities in the company's retail stores throughout the country. Information on retail positions is also available at (800) 558-0206, ext. 4395.

Toys "R" Us

http://help.toysrus.com

A huge retail chain that sells toys, clothing, and equipment. There are over 700 stores in 49 states, employing more than 60,000 sales associates. Click "Career Opportunities" to learn about positions regularly available and how to apply for them.

COURSES

The Retail Employer Link to Education (RELE)
RELE Initiative
National Retail Federation
325 7th Street NW, Suite 1100
Washington, DC 20004
(202) 783-7971
The RELE is the National Retail Federation's school-to-career program, which offers hands-on opportunities for young people to explore careers in retailing through state retail associations in Arizona, Hawaii, Iowa, Maryland, New Mexico, Texas, and Illinois.

Retail Skills Center
Downtown Seattle Association
500 Union Street, Suite 325
Seattle, WA 98101
(206) 625-9940
Working in partnership with Seattle community colleges, the center provides education and training programs for people who want to begin careers in the retail industry.

BOOKS

Groveman, Shelly Field. *Career Opportunities in the Retail and Wholesale Industry*. New York: Facts on File, 2001.
A comprehensive look at more than seventy careers in retailing, including sections on specialty stores, malls, and shopping centers.

VIDEOS

Career Kids
5043 Gregg Way
Auburn, CA 95602
(800) 537-0909
Web site: http://www.careerkids.com
This organization offers an excellent selection of brief occupational videos you can watch on your computer for free, including one on working in retail.

10

SCHOOL BUS DRIVER

If you like driving, enjoy children, and would like to have summers and school vacations off, you may want to be a school bus driver. School bus drivers are usually assigned set routes, which they cover every school day, Monday to Friday. The route includes specific stops and the time the bus is expected to arrive at each of those points. Drivers are often assigned two routes, perhaps to deliver high school students between 7:00 AM and 8:00 AM, then pick up elementary school students and deliver them to their school between 8:00 AM and 9:00 AM. In this case, the driver is also likely to be assigned two routes in the afternoon, returning the same two groups of students to their homes.

Many drivers work twenty hours or less a week, bringing children to school in the morning and home in the afternoon. Some drivers increase their earnings by accepting assignments to take children on field trips or to athletic events.

Unlike public transit bus drivers, school bus drivers do not have to collect fares from their passengers, although in some school districts they are required to check that students have bus passes. They must, however, attend to paperwork. This usually involves completing weekly reports on the number of students transported, the number of "runs" completed, the amount of miles traveled, and how much fuel was consumed.

While some bus companies house all their buses at a central depot or garage, others allow bus drivers who have adequate parking space to take their buses home with them at night. This saves time and eliminates the need for transportation to get to and from the depot.

School bus drivers perform an important service that requires a high degree of responsibility. They need to be able to block out distractions and pay careful attention to their

These children are boarding a school bus. School bus drivers must be able to monitor the behavior of the students on the bus without being distracted from driving safely.

driving, particularly in poor weather. Extra caution is required each time children get on and off the bus.

Drivers must also enforce the safety standards set by their school district. Usually this means taking care to allow only students to board the bus. To further guarantee safety, they need to be able to control the behavior of their passengers. When children are disruptive or loud, they can distract a driver and put all the passengers in jeopardy. A good school bus driver does not tolerate disruptive behavior. By communicating with school and bus company officials when problems arise, and quickly addressing those problems, a responsible driver can ably ensure the safety of young passengers.

Schools serve children who have a broad variety of physical, mental, and behavioral disabilities, and school bus drivers need to learn how to meet the needs of these special passengers. If you decide to become a school bus driver and go for interviews with several different employers, be sure to ask them what kind of training drivers receive to help them accommodate children who have special needs.

In communities that own their own fleet of buses, drivers are employed by the school district. But in about one-third of the nation's school districts, the school system contracts with an outside bus company to provide transportation for its students. In this case, the driver is an employee of the bus company. Either way, some drivers increase their working hours and their paychecks by making themselves available for extra assignments, like taking children on field trips or to athletic events.

Education and Training

Employers want to see a good driving record and most require a high school diploma. In some states, a background check is required before you can be hired as a school bus driver. That's to ensure that drivers have no history of criminal activity or mental illness. Potential drivers are also usually subjected to drug and alcohol testing prior to employment. Some systems continue random testing after employment.

To become a school bus driver, you must also be in good physical condition, free of any chronic diseases that could reduce your ability to drive safely. Good vision (with or without corrective lenses) is also a requirement. Plus, you must be strong enough to comfortably drive the bus.

You must hold a commercial driver's license from the state you live in to be hired as a school bus driver. Because many drivers have never driven a vehicle anywhere near as large as a school bus, training is provided by the employer. Depending on state and local regulations, you will participate in a one- to four-week training program that includes both driving and classroom instruction. You will become familiar with the features of the bus you will drive, and you will have

A school bus driver shares a light moment with a student before he exits the bus. The driver must pay attention to the special needs of each child.

the opportunity to practice driving it with an experienced driver aboard. You will learn about safe driving practices, emergency evacuation procedures, first aid, accommodating special-needs students, proper driver-student relations, and the laws and school policies that govern the operation of school buses in the area in which you work.

Salary

According to the US census, the median hourly wage for school bus drivers was $10.67 in 2000. Because of the part-time nature of their work, many school bus drivers do not receive health and dental insurance, pension plans, or other benefits. However, some school systems do offer benefits, so it is wise to compare several potential employers.

Outlook

In 2000, approximately 444,000 people worked as school bus drivers. Employment prospects are bright through 2010 because the school population in the United States is growing, particularly in the suburbs.

Consider These Facts:

- School buses are nearly 2,000 times safer than the family car.

- Every year, 440,000 public school buses travel 4.3 billion miles to transport 23.5 million children to and from school and school-related activities.

- The school bus is the only mode of transportation that has reduced the incidence of accidents, injuries, and fatalities while increasing the number of vehicles, miles, and passengers annually.

(Source: The National School Transportation Association)

FOR MORE INFORMATION

ASSOCIATIONS

National Association for Pupil Transportation
1840 Western Avenue
Albany, NY 12203
(800) 989-6278
Web site: http://www.napt.org
This professional membership organization strives to improve all aspects of student transportation.

National School Transportation Association (NSTA)
Web site: http://www.schooltrans.com
The NSTA is a trade organization for companies that own and operate school buses.

Regional Transportation and Safety Institute
Web site: http://www.kresanet.org/kresa/transportation/busdriver.htm
This is a good place to learn about the components of safety education programs for beginning drivers.

For information on school bus driver requirements specific to your state, contact the nearest office of the Department of Motor Vehicles.

WEB SITES

North Carolina Department of Motor Vehicles
http://www.dmv.dot.state.nc.us/schoolbusandtrafficsafety
At the School Bus and Traffic Safety section of the North Carolina DMV Web site, you will find the forty-six-page *School Bus Driver's Handbook,* containing everything you need to know about safe bus operation and the supervision of passengers. It is full of tests you can take to check your understanding of the material.

Public Transportation Safety Institute
http://www.ptsi.org/catalog.htm
The Public Transportation Safety Institute produced the PTSI Resource Catalog, an online source that lists dozens of products related to school bus safety and driver training.

School Bus Information Council
http://www.schoolbusinfo.org
This site provides statistics and background information for reporters covering school bus issues and accidents. The organization also runs a toll-free hotline where experts on school bus subjects stand ready to answer questions.

BOOKS

J. J. Keller & Associates. *Keller's School Bus Driver's Safety Handbook*. Neenah, WI: J. J. Keller & Associates, Inc., 2002.
This books discusses forty different topics, including passenger safety, avoiding dangerous situations, managing student behavior, and school zone driving.

PERIODICALS

School Bus Fleet
http://www.schoolbusfleet.com
This trade magazine covers issues of interest to drivers, including how to handle disruptive students.

VIDEOS

School Bus Driver: Positively in Control
This is a training video that explores the ways in which the attitude of the school bus driver affects safety. Distributed by the Coastal Training Technologies Corporation. The student transportation coordinator in your school district may be able to lend you a copy.

11

SCHOOL SECRETARY

Perhaps you think you know exactly what a school secretary's job involves. After all, you have spent years in school. But the fact is that many of the responsibilities associated with this job are not as readily apparent. To get an idea of all the tasks that fall to someone in this position, here is a typical job description that lists just a few of the duties noted in an advertisement for a position in Tennessee:

School Secretary:

- Reports to principal

- Has expertise in public relations work on the telephone

- Provides assistance to students, staff, parents, and visitors

- Relays and records messages accurately

- Has good typing and bookkeeping skills

- Keeps information confidential concerning school business

- Knows and follows proper procedures for the safeguarding of pupil personal information

- Maintains a complete and systematic set of records

- Prepares financial statements and cost reports

- Locates and removes requested information

- Complies with federal, state, and local regulations, as well as school board policies and administrative regulations

And that is only half the list!

Working as a school secretary is a job that combines good people skills with an ability to keep track of detailed information. The larger the school you work in, the busier the office. Your responsibility is to help make the school run smoothly. You will have a great deal of contact with both students and adults, and you will assume important responsibilities.

School secretaries typically pick up all the loose ends that go with life in a school setting. Although the specific things you do in the course of a day will vary according to whether you work in an elementary, middle, or high school, the tasks will always be varied. If you are in an elementary school, in addition to your regular duties you might find yourself working with vendors to set up a book fair. In a middle school or high school, you might be asked to help organize a health fair.

Successful school secretaries are polite and pleasant, yet firm. They can function well in a frequently hectic environment. They are well organized and calm in the face of crisis.

School secretaries must also respect the confidential nature of some of the information they handle. School secretaries know which children are under the care of the department of social services, and which ones live in a shelter or a foster home. They also know which children are involved in custody disputes. They do their best to protect the privacy of each student.

A school secretary updates information in an elementary school's computer database.

As gatekeeper of the principal's office, a school secretary is the first person many parents and visitors meet when they enter the school. School secretaries also encounter newcomers to the community who want to enroll their children, supply salesmen, newspaper reporters in search of a story, and police officers looking for a particular youngster. They need to make certain that each person is treated appropriately and with respect.

In addition, school secretaries sometimes encounter angry parents who demand to see the principal or a specific teacher immediately. They need to know how to react to these parents in a way that calms rather than escalates the situation. They also encounter adults, including parents without custody of their children, who want to have a child dismissed, but who are not listed on the child's emergency form. In situations like these, school secretaries become part of the team effort that schools put forward to assure the safety of each child.

If you want a career working with children where you will be respected for both your competence in managing detailed information and your ability to work well with all kinds of people, a position as a school secretary might be right for you.

Education and Training

Although a high school diploma is the only educational requirement for many school secretary positions, computer skills and experience working in a busy office are highly valued. Some positions require that candidates be able to type fifty words per minute. Taking business courses in high school or at a community college can also help you to land a job. Experience working with children, perhaps as a camp counselor, Sunday school teacher, or volunteer coach, is also valued.

Many skills are acquired through on-the-job training. If the state mandates a new method of keeping track of standardized test scores, the school secretary may be sent to workshops to learn to use the software required to do the job. In addition, many school systems offer in-house courses on how to use popular software programs like Excel or PowerPoint.

Salary

According to the U.S. 2000 census, half of the people working as school secretaries in 2000 earned above $23,870 and half earned below that amount. Those who work year-round (usually high school positions) earn more than those who have the summers off. School secretaries usually receive excellent benefits. In many school districts, secretaries belong to a union that advocates for regular pay raises.

Outlook

Nearly 25 percent of all Americans are enrolled in educational institutions. Educational services is the largest industry in the country, providing nearly 12 million jobs. About 10 percent of these positions are as school secretaries, administrative assistants, and clerks.

Pam Sweet, School Secretary

Pam Sweet is the secretary at Fuller Elementary School in Gloucester, Massachusetts, the town where she grew up. Immediately after graduating from Gloucester High School, she went to work as a bookkeeper. Pam later attended a one-year secretarial course and taught herself basic computer skills. Since she has always enjoyed being around children, she eventually decided to go to work as a school secretary.

Q: What kind of person makes a good elementary school secretary?

A: You need to be understanding and nurturing. There are so many people involved in the daily life of a school—staff, outside counselors, administrators, teachers, psychologists, children, and parents from all walks of life. You need to be pleasant and have a smile for all of them.

It also helps to have a lot of common sense and to be comfortable making decisions about what's OK and what's not OK, like when a child can use the school phone and when he or she can't. There are 646 students in my school. It's a very, very busy place.

Q: What's a typical day like in your job?

A: Well, the phone never stops ringing. There are tons of interruptions. I might have a project I plan to accomplish, but the priorities change by the minute. You have to be extremely flexible.

I start out each morning working with the computer program that keeps track of attendance. The program has thirty-five different types of data that the state requires us to keep track of for every student, so I'm constantly updating that information. And I do all the Department of Education reports.

I take messages for all of the staff throughout the day and I handle phone calls from parents who call for lots of different reasons. One might want to know if her child arrived at school safely. Another wants to know if it's a field trip day. Another is worried because her daughter forgot her homework or her lunch.

Also, children are being dismissed at all times of the day. I need to know who's picking them up and to make sure that that person is listed on their emergency form.

Q: What's the worst part of your job?

A: The worst is seeing a child that needs a lot of help because of his or her life situation and knowing there's nothing I can do. It makes me very sad when I just cannot bring a smile to a child's face.

Q: What's the best part of your job?

A: The very, very best thing is when I'm sitting at my desk working and a first grader comes in and says, "I just want you to know, Mrs. Sweet, I'm having a really great day."

FOR MORE INFORMATION

ASSOCIATIONS

National Association of Educational Office Professionals
P.O. Box 12619
Wichita, KS 67277-2619
(316) 942-4822
Web site: http://www.naeop.org
Provides academic programs and conferences for people who work in school offices and who want to grow professionally. Awards a series of certificates based on education, experience, and professional activity.

National Education Association (NEA)
1201 16th Street NW
Washington, DC 20036
(202) 833-4000
Web site: http://www.nea.org
Membership in the NEA is open to people who work in public schools.

WEB SITES

Strawberry Point School Disaster Preparedness Plan
http://www.mvschools.org/sp/disaster_plan.htm
Details the role of the school secretary and other school staff in the event that a particular school district's emergency plan is activated.

TeacherWeb.com
http://www.teacherweb.com
A very chatty, friendly site with lots of information about people who work in schools.

Tuscaloosa City Schools
http://www.tusc.k12.al.us
This site of the Tuscaloosa, Alabama, city school system includes detailed job descriptions for a high school secretary, a child nutrition program secretary, an attendance and health secretary, a special education secretary, and more.

BOOKS

Casanova, Ursula. *Elementary School Secretaries: The Women in the Principal's Office*. Thousand Oaks, CA: Corwin Press, 1992.

Fatooh, Audrey, and Barbara Mauk. *The Secretary: A Manual of Writing Style and Handbook of Business English for Education Secretaries*. Palm Springs, CA: Etc Publications, 1997.
Very detailed coverage of all the problems a school secretary is likely to face.

Priest, Jean L. *The Effective Education Secretary* (Effective School Administration Series, Number 2). Palm Springs, CA: Etc Publications, 1989.
Easy-to-understand text gets right to the point.

12

TEACHER ASSISTANT

Picture yourself spending your workday in a school setting, immersed in an atmosphere charged with energy and filled with activity. In the course of one day you might find yourself maintaining attendance records, working one-on-one with a child who needs some extra help, and keeping your eye on thirty children in the cafeteria. All of these tasks help to make the day move smoothly for the teacher or teachers to whom you have been assigned. That is what being a teacher assistant is all about.

If you are patient and even-tempered, like the idea of working in a school, enjoy spending time with children, and are attracted to the idea of a school vacation schedule, this may be a good position to explore.

Approximately 40 percent of teacher assistants work part-time. Some work only two or three hours a day, while others work a full school day when school is in session. Teacher assistants sometimes work outside, supervising recesses or accompanying students on field trips. Depending upon their specific assignments, they might spend a large amount of time on their feet.

There are many types of teacher assistants, depending on whether the job is located in an elementary, middle, or high school. The responsibilities of the job also vary widely. In an elementary school setting, some teacher assistants are hired for a specific task such as supervising lunch sessions or playground time. Others are hired to provide extra attention, working with children individually or in small groups under the direction of a classroom teacher.

In middle schools and high schools, teacher assistants are sometimes called teacher aides or instructional aides. Their responsibilities tend to be more specialized than those who work with younger children. For example, if you enjoy technology, you might want to search for a teacher assistant position working in a computer lab, helping students learn to use software and helping them find the information they need for their assignments. Or you could be hired to schedule and operate audiovisual equipment, including VCRs, slide projectors, and camcorders.

Another major area of specialization for teacher assistants is special education. The trend in education over the past decade has been to include children with special needs in the regular classroom setting whenever possible. For some children, a teacher assistant is what makes this possible. A child with a severe physical disability may be assigned a teacher assistant to help him with everything from getting from one classroom to another to feeding and personal care. A child with severe behavioral problems might require an assistant to help her manage her aggression so that she can function in a regular classroom without disrupting her classmates. Teacher assistants are also assigned to provide support for children for whom English is a second language and for children who simply need extra help or homework assistance.

A teacher assistant shows a student how to use a computer program.

A teacher assistant can make a significant contribution to the well-being of one child or a group of children. Often it is the assistant who spends the most time with a child who is having difficulty. He or she can help the teacher assess the child's progress and suggest lessons that might work well with that particular child. An assistant who is involved with a group of children, perhaps working in a classroom or supervising a "time-out" room for kids who have misbehaved, contributes to the orderly atmosphere of a school, making it a better place for teachers to teach and children to learn.

Education and Training

To become a teacher assistant, you must hold a high school diploma or a GED. Many school systems also require some college work, usually courses in child development.

Community colleges often offer two-year associate's degree programs that prepare students for jobs as teacher assistants. Some states require that teacher assistants pass a basic skills test while other states require certification. But no matter what level of preparation they bring to the job, teacher assistants almost always receive on-the-job training.

The more training you have, the more likely you are to be able to find a position as a classroom assistant that involves hands-on instruction such as tutoring or reviewing homework.

Nonteaching positions, such as those involving supervision outside the classroom (in the cafeteria, playground, parking lot, and so on), require less training. Employers also look for prior experience working with children. If you have held a position as a counselor at a summer camp, assisted at a day care center, or volunteered to help coach a youth team, be certain to mention this experience on your application or résumé.

Once you have secured a position as a teacher assistant, opportunities to advance are usually dependent upon acquiring more education. Some school systems offer their employees tuition assistance to help them improve and expand their skills.

Salary

According to the 2000 census, in 2000, half of the teacher assistants in the United States earned under $17,350 and half earned above that. Those who work full-time usually receive health insurance and other benefits, while those who work part-time do not usually receive any benefits.

Outlook

Because of the teacher shortage anticipated over the next decade, opportunities for teaching assistants are expected to grow. The demand will be greatest in those areas experiencing an increase in population and school enrollments. Applicants who speak a second language, particularly Spanish, will be in high demand because bilingual teacher assistants play an important role in communicating with students and families whose primary language is not English. The number of teacher assistant positions focused on working with special-needs students is expected to increase as federal laws continue to emphasize including children with physical, emotional, and learning disabilities in a regular classroom setting.

As with many occupations that require minimal training and offer relatively low wages, turnover among teacher assistants is high, creating a regular stream of job openings. New opportunities for teacher assistants are also expected to develop as an increasing number of school systems establish after-school and summer programs for their students as additional tools for helping to improve student performance.

Terms You Should Know

Instructional aide This term is used interchangeably with "teacher assistant."

Paraeducator This term applies to all nonprofessional employees who work in a school setting and includes teacher assistants, teacher aides, and instructional aides.

Paraprofessional This term applies to employees who assist professionals. Teacher aides, teacher assistants, instructional aides, and paraeducators all fall into this category, as do school secretaries and library aides.

Teacher aide In some states, this term is used interchangeably with "teacher assistant," but in other states it refers to employees who assist the teacher by performing nonteaching duties that would otherwise be performed by the teacher. These duties include record keeping, preparing materials and equipment, and attending to the physical needs of students.

Teacher assistant A person who holds this position provides instructional and clerical help to one or more teachers.

FOR MORE INFORMATION

For specific information about requirements and opportunities for becoming a teacher assistant where you live, contact your state department of education and the superintendent's office in your local school district.

ASSOCIATIONS

American Federation of Teachers
Paraprofessional and School-Related Personnel Division
555 New Jersey Avenue NW
Washington, DC 20001
(800) 238-1133, ext. 4696
Web site: http://www.aft.org/psrp
Provides information on teacher assistant training and certification. Request the brochure *Your Career as an Education Paraprofessional* and a sample copy of *PSRP Reporter*, a quarterly newsletter that covers issues of importance to paraprofessionals.

National Resource Center for Paraprofessionals
6526 Old Main Hill
Utah State University
Logan, UT 84322
(435) 797-7272
Web site: http://www.nrcpara.org

WEB SITES

National Teacher Recruitment Clearinghouse

http://www.recruitingteachers.org

Hosted by the National Teacher Recruitment Clearinghouse, this Web site has a section called "Teacher Aide." It also includes links to the department of education in each state.

Research & Educational Services—New York State United Teachers

http://www.nysut.org/research/bulletins/
20010401teacheraides.html

This site contains a summary of the New York State laws, rules, and regulations that govern the employment of teacher aides (who perform only nonteaching duties) and teacher assistants (who provide direct instructional assistance to students) in New York State. New York requires that teacher assistants are certified, and this Web site explains what is needed for certification.

BOOKS

Long, Carol. *Piecing Together the Paraprofessional Puzzle*. Columbia, MO: University of Missouri-Columbia, 1996.
Instructional Media Laboratory
University of Missouri-Columbia
Columbia, MO 65211
(800) 669-2465
This handbook is directed toward issues faced by the first-year teacher assistant. It explains the roles and functions of the position.

Rush, Karen. *Early Childhood: The Role of the Paraprofessional* (Student Edition). Minneapolis, MN: The University of Minnesota, 1995.
This publication focuses on training teacher assistants to address the early childhood needs of children with disabilities.

VIDEOS

Beyond the Sandbox: Teaching Assistants in Early Childhood Education
Institute for the Study of Developmental Disabilities and the Indiana
Department of Education
CeDIR
2853 East 10th Street
Bloomington, IN 47408-2602
This professional development tape helps administrators and parents
understand the role played by teaching assistants.

What Do I Do Now?
Hope, Inc.
55 East 100 North, Suite 203
Logan, UT 84321
A set of twenty-four videos, these tapes introduce teacher assistants
to strategies for helping children who find it difficult to communicate.

GLOSSARY

bookmobile A large van or truck stocked with books and other materials that travels to day care centers, schools, and youth clubs that do not have their own libraries.

caregiver The person who is responsible for the well-being of a child during a particular period of time.

certification Evidence of achievement of a particular level of expertise in a particular area ranging from child care to coaching.

child development The process through which a child acquires mental, physical, social, and emotional skills.

client The person who is receiving human services.

confidentiality Protecting someone's privacy.

direct services Work that involves ongoing contact with the person who is being taught or assisted.

enrichment activities Opportunities for children to learn new skills and concepts, and explore their creativity in areas like dance, music, theater, and the visual arts.

indirect services Work that involves arranging, evaluating, or otherwise providing a particular type of assistance needed by an individual.

in-service training Courses, workshops, or other forms of education provided by one's employer.

language skills Abilities related to using, understanding, and pronouncing words.

limit setting Establishing rules concerning behavior and the consequences that will occur when those rules are broken.

listening stations Individual desks or tables set up in a classroom or library with earphones and a tape or CD player, where a child can independently hear a story or music.

residential facility A place where people live who need the kind of assistance and support that cannot be provided in their home.

role model Someone who serves as a positive example.

special education Programs designed to provide assistance to help children address physical, mental, emotional, and behavioral difficulties that make it difficult for them to learn.

special needs Physical, mental, emotional, and social difficulties experienced by some children that make it difficult for them to learn.

versatility The ability to adjust one's performance or teaching approach to meet the needs of a particular individual or audience.

INDEX

About the Author

Harriet Webster, the author of fifteen books, lives in Gloucester, Massachusetts.

Photo Credits

Cover © Joseph Poellot/Index Stock; pp. 7, 9 © Mike Kirkpatrick/Index Stock; p. 12 © Mark Segal/Index Stock; pp. 18, 21 © Tony Freeman/Index Stock; pp. 23, 29, 32, 106, 108 © Index Stock; pp. 34, 64, 67 © Corbis; pp. 41, 46 © Robert Holmes/Corbis; p. 43 © Owen Franklen/Corbis; pp. 52, 58–59 © Mitch Diamond/Index Stock; p. 54 © Jaye Phillips/Index Stock; pp. 73, 75 © Stewart Cohen/Index Stock; p. 78 © Jim McGuire/Index Stock; pp. 84, 87 © Catherine Karnow/Corbis; p. 89 © Patrick Ward/Corbis; pp. 96, 98 © John Bazemore/AP/Wide World Photos; p. 111 © Dann Tardif/Corbis; pp. 115, 118 © Chip Henderson/ Index Stock; pp. 126, 129 © Paul Barton/Corbis.

Editor

Jill Jarnow

Series Design

Evelyn Horovicz

Layout

Nelson Sá